Samuel Wheelwright

A new system of instruction in the Indian club exercise

Containing a simple and accurate explanation of all the graceful motions

Samuel Wheelwright

A new system of instruction in the Indian club exercise
Containing a simple and accurate explanation of all the graceful motions

ISBN/EAN: 9783337120559

Printed in Europe, USA, Canada, Australia, Japan

Cover: Foto ©Andreas Hilbeck / pixelio.de

More available books at **www.hansebooks.com**

A NEW SYSTEM

OF

INSTRUCTION

IN THE

INDIAN CLUB EXERCISE;

CONTAINING

A SIMPLE AND ACCURATE EXPLANATION OF ALL THE GRACEFUL
MOTIONS AS PRACTISED BY GYMNASTS, PUGILISTS, ETC.

BY

SAMUEL T. WHEELWRIGHT.

ILLUSTRATED WITH TEN BACK-VIEW PLATES.

TORONTO:

THE CANADIAN NEWS AND PUBLISHING CO.

1871.

A NEW SYSTEM

OF

INSTRUCTION

IN THE

INDIAN CLUB EXERCISE;

CONTAINING

A SIMPLE AND ACCURATE EXPLANATION OF ALL THE GRACEFUL
MOTIONS AS PRACTISED BY GYMNASTS, PUGILISTS, ETC.

BY

SAMUEL T. WEELWRIGHT.

ILLUSTRATED WITH TEN BACK-VIEW PLATES.

TORONTO:
THE CANADIAN NEWS AND PUBLISHING CO.
1871.

SAMUEL T. WHEELWRIGHT'S

INSTRUCTIONS

IN THE

INDIAN CLUB EXERCISE.

INDIAN CLUBS within the last few years have become the most popular method of developing the muscles of the body, and keeping it in a healthy and vigorous state. For in-door exercise there is nothing that can compete with them, the exercise far excelling the tedious motions required in using Dumb-Bells, Pulley-Weights, &c., they being the same thing over and over again ; while, with clubs, new motions, changes, and combinations are continually entering the mind, making it a source of pleasure, as well as benefiting the system. All persons whose avocations are of a sedentary nature should devote a portion of their time each day to this exercise, in the morning after rising, and at their place of business, after business hours; and they will soon find themselves instilled with new life, and that labor, instead of being a burden, will become a pleasure. These are facts, and something which all sensible persons will admit.

The author is aware there has been wanting one very important thing, and that is, a cheap and simple work on instruction in the art of club-swinging, thus enabling all classes to possess themselves of it ; and, believing himself capable in every way of giving a simple and accurate description of all the most important motions, taking particular care to word it in such a manner that it may be easily understood by all, he respectfully submits this work to all those that wish to perfect themselves in this art.

We will give our first attention to the motions with the single club, it being very necessary to learn these thoroughly first, as the motions with double clubs are merely a combination of them.

You will perceive by the Plates, that the figure in each is represented standing with the back towards the reader, for the purpose of more clearly explaining the motions ; enabling the learner, while holding the engraving before him in one hand, to follow the course of the club in the engraving with the other, without reversing the motion, which would be necessary if the figure faced the reader.   This method makes this the simplest work in existence, and all persons who have undertaken to learn from other works will appreciate its value.

POSITION.

If convenient, toe a line on the floor; if not, imagine yourself toeing one ; and I would wish particularly to impress upon your mind that, in most all of the motions with clubs, both single and double, the clubs are kept, while in motion parallel with this line.   This is very necessary, as it adds greatly to the gracefulness of the motions.   The heels a few inches apart, the feet well spread; stand in an easy position, with the chest extended and chin slightly raised, the left arm hanging by the side; the club within the right hand, with the knuckles outwards, and the hand opposite the right breast and a few inches from it, with the club perpendicular; the elbow close to the side, the body should be kept square to the front. In all of the following motions, it will be understood, you are to start from this position.

THE WREATH.

This is one of the most important motions, it being necessary to execute this in a great many of the others. You commence by raising the right hand till it arrives about three inches above the centre of the head, the club leaning slightly towards the left; the dropping the club behind the back, pointing to the left, being careful to keep it parallel or pointing in the same direction with the line, and allowing it to describe a circle behind your back, the centre being your hand, which moves from the top of your hand to the back of your neck. Do not hang on to the club as if you were afraid of dropping it, but when you start the circle give the club a jerk, and let the force and its weight carry it around the circle. As the circle is nearly terminated, you twist your wrist to the right to keep the club parallel with the line, and then bring it over the right shoulder, stopping when the hand reaches its former position—that is, opposite the right breast.

Do not at any time allow the hand to go below the shoulder. After learning it with the right, change to the left.

Do not imagine, after you have executed it a few times, you are master of it ; for, after trying one or two of the other motions, you will be very likely to forget it.

In the engraving (Plate I.), Figure 1 represents the position of the body and the clubs, and Fig. 2 the position of the hand while executing the Wreath, the course of the club being shown by the dotted lines.

Fig. 1.

Fig. 2

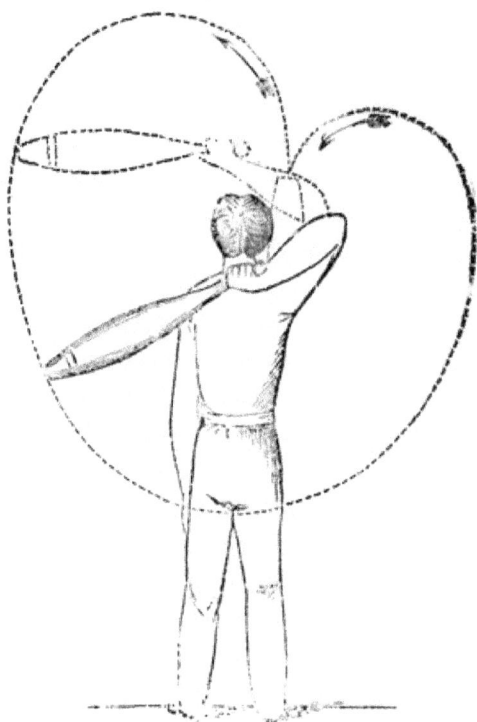

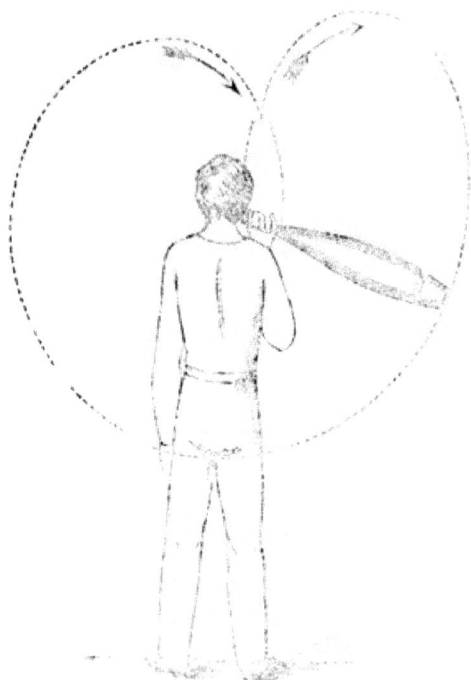

PLATE II.

the
the
me
the
and
cle
an
it

THE SHOULDER TWIST.

Raise the hand till it arrives opposite the right ear, and then twisting the wrist so that the thumb will be directly to the right, and dropping the club towards the right behind the shoulder, releasing the club with the three last fingers, merely holding it with the forefinger and thumb parallel with the line, the hand moving a little below and back of the ear, and keeping it in that position, thus allowing the club to clear the shoulder, giving it a jerk as described in the Wreath, and allowing it to describe a circle, twisting the wrist to keep it on the line as the club passes around. At the end of the circle bring the hand back to the starting point.

Plate II. shows the position of the hand and club while executing the circle.

THE HEAD CIRCLE.

Raise the hand and club perpendicularly at arm's length, knuckles to the right, and swing the club at arm's length to the left, parallel with the line describing a circle in front of the body, the right shoulder being the centre, giving it a jerk as before, keeping the body square to the front. When the hand reaches the position in which it was when the circle was first started—that is, at arm's length above the head— you drop the club to the left, at the same time allowing the hand to fall to the back of the neck, and then describe a circle behind the back, (this last circle, you will perceive, is the Wreath); then let the hand and club be again extended at arm's length, not perpendicularly, but in more of a circle, to make it look graceful, and then execute the first circle over again ; making, as you will see by the engraving, a continuous line and a circle within a circle.

Learn this thoroughly with both hands ; with the left start the club towards the right.

Plate III. shows the position of the hand and club while starting the large circle.

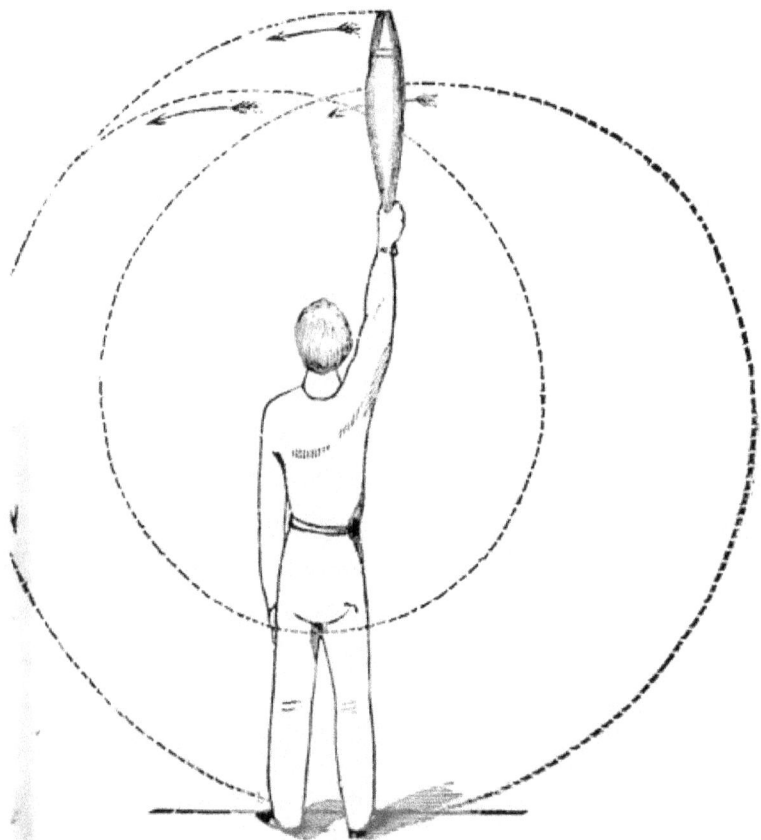

PLATE III.

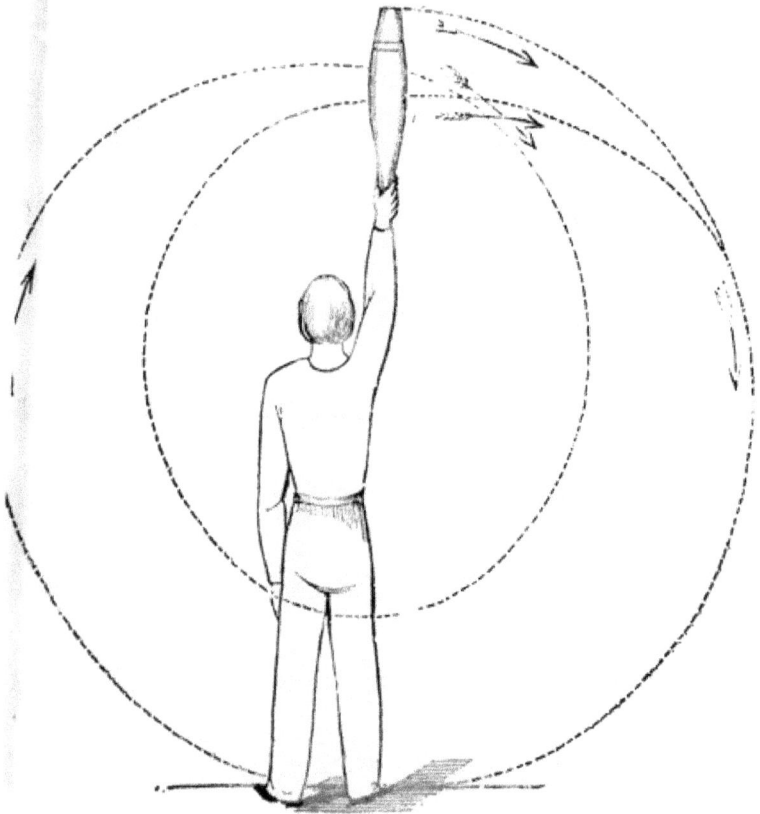

PLATE IV.

THE SHOULDER CIRCLE.

Raise the club perpendicularly at arm's length as before, knuckles to the rear, and swing the club at arm's length to th right, parallel with the line describing a circle in front of the body, the shoulder being the centre, giving it a jerk as before, keeping the body square to the front. When the hand reaches the position it was when the circle was first started—that is, at arm's length above the head,—you twist your wrist, bringing your thumb to the right, and let the club drop behind the shoulder, the hand dropping at the same time below and back of the ear, releasing the club with the three last fingers, merely holding it with the forefinger and thumb, the club describing a circle, (this, you will recognize, is the Shoulder Twist); then let the hand and club be again extended at arm's length, not perpendicularly, but more towards the right, and then execute the first circle over again: making, as in the last motion (the Head Circle), a continuous line and a circle within a circle.

Learn thoroughly with both hands; with the left start the club towards the left.

Plate IV. shows the position of the hand and club while starting the large circle.

EXTENSION.

This, as a single club motion, is not as graceful as the others, but with two clubs makes a very pretty one. You commence by raising the hand till it arrives about three inches above the centre of the head, the club leaning slightly towards the left : then dropping the club behind the back pointing to the left, not forgetting to keep it parallel with the line, the hand moving at the same time from the top of the head to the back of the neck, and allowing the club to describe a circle (this, so far, you will perceive is the same as the Wreath); but when the club arrives to the position (pointing downwards) parallel with and opposite to your right leg, you quickly twist your wrist and bring your elbow to the front, letting the hand move towards the ear, raising the club so that it will point directly to the right, without altering the position of your hand, and then extend your hand and club horizontally at arm's length to the right ; you then drop the club towards the floor, keeping the arm and club extended, swinging the club in a circle towards the left in front of the body, and, when it reaches the left shoulder, bring the hand to the position three inches above the head, keeping the club horizontal, and then execute the Wreath and the rest of the above motion over again.

Learn this thoroughly with both hands ; with the left start the club towards the right.

Plate V. shows the position of the hand and club at arm's length to the right. Plate IX. shows the motion with the left hand.

These five motions that I have just explained are the five principal motions with clubs, all the double motions being a

raceful as th
ty one. Yo
s about thre
aning slightl
ind the back
rallel with th
the top of th
e c'ub to de
s the same a
the position
osite to you
g your elbow
e ear, raising
ight, without
nd your hand
ht ; you then
rm and club
s the left in
eft shoulder,
ve the head.
the Wreath

the left start

lub at arm's
on with the

are the five
ons being a

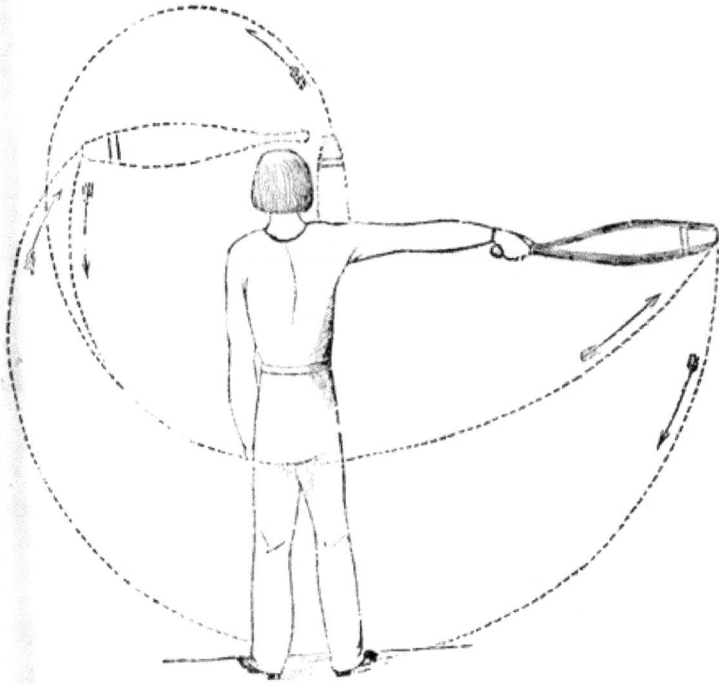

PLATE V.

coul
twist
call
that
whic
to co

W
all o
diffi
hanc
this
and
they
one
follc

T
the
the
wil

combination of them. There are, of course, a number of
twists with the wrists and changes of the body, which some
call motions; but after you have thoroughly learned these
that I have written, the others will soon come to you, and
which I do not consider distinct motions, and will only tend
to confuse instead of benefiting the learner.

We will now proceed with the double motions. In almost
all of these motions there is one thing you will find very
difficult to overcome at first: that is, a tendency for the one
hand to follow the other. You have, of course, noticed by
this time that, in executing the single motions with the right
and left hands, the club moves in opposite directions, which
they also do in the double motions, moving independent of
one another; hence the difficulty of keeping them from
following one another.

The position of the body is the same. Remember the line;
the left-hand club is held in the same position as the right,
the left hand opposite the left breast : and this position, it
will be understood, is the starting point of all these motions.

THE DOUBLE WREATH.

Start the right-hand club as explained in the single Wreath,
and follow with the left when the right hand reaches the
back of the neck, keeping up a continuous circle, not bringing
the hands back to the breasts, but executing the motion al-
ternately, first right, then left, quickly. You may, if you
wish, bring the hands back to the position opposite the
breasts at the end of each circle ; but this will have to be

done much slower than the other. (See Plate VI.) The
motion is performed both ways. This is considered one of
the best motions for developing the muscles.

Plate VI. represents the position of the hands and clubs
while in motion, stopping at the end of each circle.

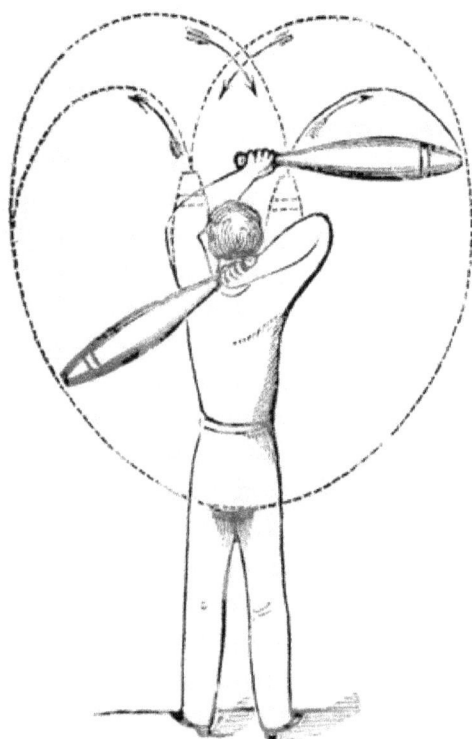

PLATE VI.

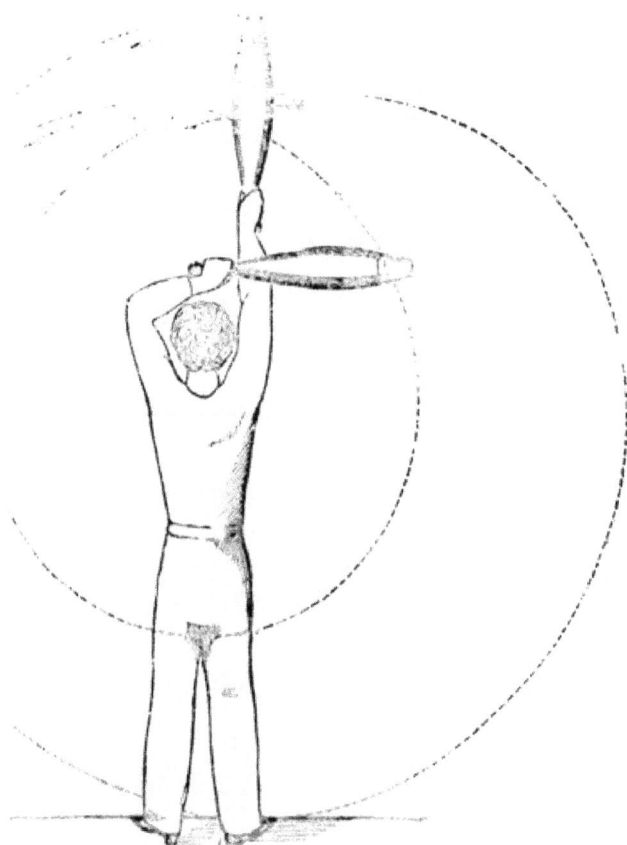

PLATE VII.

THE SHOULDER TWIST.

This is not considered a double motion, and is only used in combination with other motions.

THE DOUBLE HEAD CIRCLE.

In this motion you will find the difficulty I spoke of, in keeping the clubs apart. Start the right as explained in the single motion (Plate III.), at the same time executing the latter part of the motion first (that is, the Wreath) with the left, and then connecting it with the large circle. Thus you see that one hand has the start of the other, and moves independent of it. If you practise this well you will soon get the "knack" of keeping the clubs apart, and will help you considerably in performing the other motions.

Plate VII. shows the position of the hands and clubs as they start.

In this and all of the following engravings you will notice I have not shown the course of the left-hand club, merely showing the position of the hands when the motion is started, for the reason that, as both are the same with the left and right, except moving in different directions, it would tend to confuse the learner. If you have been careful to learn the single motion with the left as well as the right hand, you will find it very easy to comprehend the description given.

THE DOUBLE SHOULDER CIRCLE.

Start the right hand club as explained in the single Shoulder Circle, Plate IV., and at the same time execute the latter part of the motion first (that is, the Shoulder Twist) with the left hand, and then connecting it with the large circle. In this motion the learner is very apt to face a little to the left and right, but there is no necessity of doing so, and great care should be taken to avoid it, as so doing throws the clubs off the line.

Plate VIII. shows the position of the hands and clubs as they start.

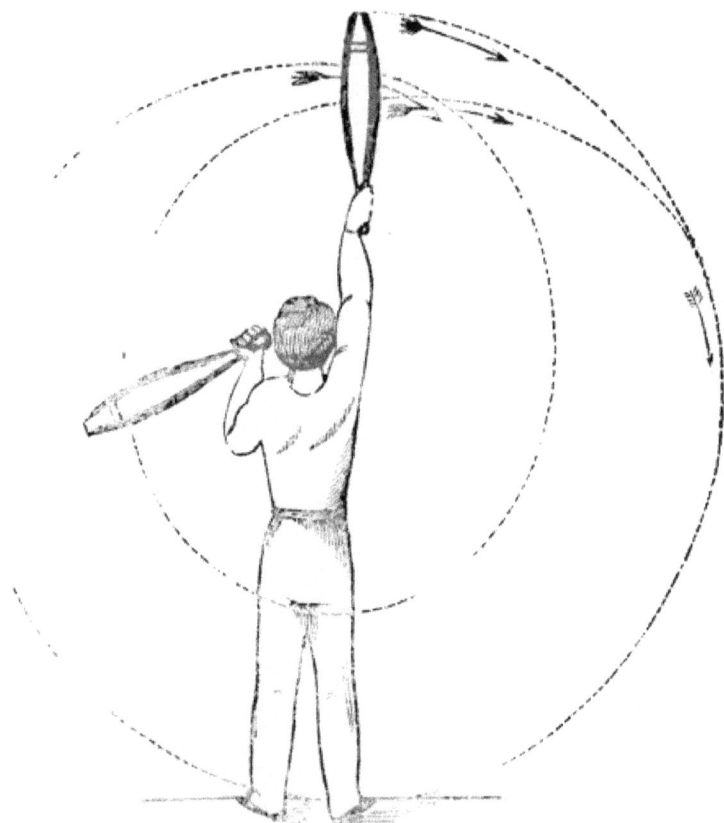

PLATE VIII.

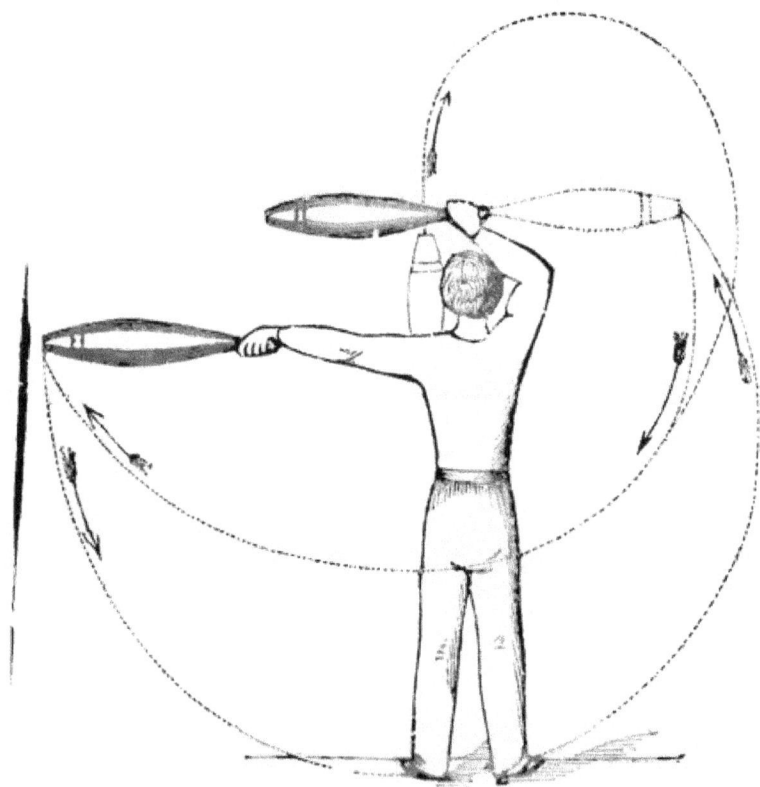

PLATE IX.

in t
as t
ext(
the
dro]
des(
reac
not:
shif
gra(

l

THE DOUBLE EXTENSION.

Start both clubs together. The right hand commences as in the single Extension motion, keeping the club in motion as therein described, and the left hand at the same time being extended at arm's length horizontally to the left, thus placing the two clubs for a moment in a parallel position, then dropping the left-hand club towards the floor, allowing it to describe a circle in front of the body; and then, when it reaches the left shoulder, execute the Wreath. You will notice that the clubs become parallel to each other as they are shifted from one shoulder to the other. This is a pretty and graceful motion, if done well.

Plate IX. shows the position of the clubs at start.

THE WINDMILL.

This motion is considered the finest and most graceful one of any in the club exercise, the clubs, while in motion, resembling the arms of a windmill revolving. It is a combination of the Head Circle (Plate III.) and the Shoulder Circle (Plate IV.) Both clubs start together. The right hand performs the Head Circle, commencing at that part of it resembling the Wreath; that is, describing a circle back of the head, and then executing the large circle. The left hand executes the Shoulder Circle, commencing exactly as explained in the single Shoulder Circle (Plate IV.), only reversing the motion, swinging the club to the left instead of to the right, the hand following the right. Here you will find the great need of the "knack" of keeping the clubs apart, as each hand performs a distinct motion by itself. You can reverse this motion, making the clubs revolve to the right by merely changing the motions with the hands, executing the Head Circle with the left and the Shoulder Circle with the right, letting the right hand follow the left.

Plate X. shows the position of the clubs at the start.

PLATE X.

PARALLEL.

This motion is almost exactly the same as the Windmill, only, instead of allowing one club to start ahead of the other, you start both precisely at the same time and in the same direction, keeping the clubs close and parallel to each other through all the movement. It does not, to a spectator, resemble the Windmill at all. You commence by causing the right hand to execute the Head Circle and the left the Shoulder Circle, starting both exactly as explained in those motions with single clubs. Reverse it by executing the Head Circle with the left hand and the Shoulder Circle with the right.

HEAD CROSS.

Is exactly the same as the Wreath (Plate I.), only the club starts at the same time, crossing behind the head, first the right club above the left, then the left above the right, changing each time they cross.

DOUBLE CROSS.

Cross them once behind the head as before, and then swing the clubs out at arm's length to the right and left, and allowing them to describe a circle in front of the body, crossing each other at the legs, and, when they reach the head, perform the Head Cross again.

WREATH AND SHOULDER TWIST.

Execute the Wreath with the right hand and the Shoulder Twist with the left, starting both clubs together exactly.

DOUBLE WREATH AND HEAD CIRCLE.

Execute the Wreath with the left hand without stopping, and at the same time execute the Head Circle with the right, starting as explained in the single Head Circle, and when it reaches that portion of the motion which requires the execution of the Wreath, perform the Double Wreath a few times, taking pains to come in nicely, and then swing the right-hand club to the left at arm's length, again performing the Head Circle, taking care to keep the left executing the Wreath. Reverse it, letting the right hand execute the Wreath and the left the Head Circle.

SHOULDER TWIST AND HEAD CIRCLE.

Execute the Shoulder Twist with the left hand without stopping, and the Wreath a few times with the right, and then suddenly swing the right club to the left and execute the Head Circle, keeping the left performing the Shoulder Twist ; and when the right-hand club reaches that portion of the Head Circle which requires the execution of the Wreath, perform the Wreath a few times, taking pains that the clubs will come close and parallel to each other, and then again execute the Head Circle. Reverse it, letting the right hand perform the Shoulder Twist and the left the Head Circle.

WREATH AND SHOULDER CIRCLE.

Execute the Wreath with the right hand and the Shoulder Twist with the left, starting both clubs together, as explained in the descriptions of the motions. Having performed this a few times, suddenly extend the left club at arm's length and describe a circle in front of the body (keeping the right hand executing the Wreath), as explained in the Shoulder Circle ; and when the club reaches that portion of the Shoulder Circle that requires the execution of the Shoulder Twist, let the two clubs come in nicely together. This can be reversed the same as the rest.

ELBOW TWIST.

In this motion you twist the wrists, bringing the backs of the hands square to the front, throwing them each a little outwards to the right and left, keeping the elbows close into the sides, at the same time dropping both clubs straight in front of you, not allowing the hands to move from their positions, giving the clubs a jerk and causing them to describe a circle. You may start both clubs together, or you may start one ahead of the other. In this and the following motions you do not keep the clubs parallel with the line, but at right angles.

BACKWARD AND FORWARD SWING.

Let your right foot go to the rear of the left about a foot, as you require a brace in this motion. Commence by letting the clubs both together fall over the shoulders as far back as you can, bending the body to let them go well back, being careful not to touch your back or shoulders with the clubs or the hands; then give them a sudden jerk forward, sending them out at arm's length, describing a circle, and letting them go as far beyond the legs as the arms will permit; then jerk them forward again at arm's length, letting them go over the shoulders as before. You can also execute this by allowing one club a start of the other. This is a splendid exercise for the chest.

ELBOW TWIST AND THE BACKWARD AND FORWARD SWING.

Let the clubs fall over the shoulders as described above, and, after jerking them forward and when they reach a perpendicular position, you execute the Elbow Twist, and then swing them out arm's length, proceeding as above explained. Each time clubs come back from behind the shoulders, perform the Elbow Twist. These three last motions are generally executed by first facing to the left and performing them, and then facing to the right.

The learner will by this time readily see that the five first motions are the principal ones—viz.. The Wreath, Shoulder Twist, Head Circle, Shoulder Circle, and Extension—and that all the other motions are merely a combination of these; and after having become master of these with single and double clubs, you will find no difficulty in performing any other motions that any person may do; and also, with a little practice, you will be able to connect a number of these motions together, not being obliged to stop at the termination of any one motion, but to execute them one after another, making a very pretty and graceful combination.

www.ingramcontent.com/pod-product-compliance
Lightning Source LLC
Chambersburg PA
CBHW021548270326
41930CB00008B/1421